Reflections of an Ancient Oak
Ann Wangari

Cover art by Feline Graphics
www.felinegraphics.com

Published by Seraph Creative in 2017
United States / United Kingdom / South Africa / Australia
www.seraphcreative.org

Typesetting & Layout by Feline
www.felinegraphics.com

Printed in

ISBN 978-0-620-77310-2

REFLECTIONS OF AN ANCIENT OAK

ANN WANGARI

PUBLISHED BY SERAPH CREATIVE

RECOMMENDATIONS

It is such an honour to be asked to endorse this book. Anne is a delight to be around because of what she carries and who she is and I am thrilled that she has put her mystical musings into a book.

I know as you avail yourself of these writings, you will encounter Yeshua in a fresh and deeper way, as her words wash over your heart and take you to deeper realms of His love.

Anne exudes love and passion for her Saviour and you will find this same love as you read this book.

So blessed that you are part of us Anne and so proud of you.

Mamma Lindi

Ignite Hubs International

Ann Wangari has journeyed with Cabin Academy for the past 5 years.

She is a dear friend and love struck warrior poet, who has determined to be the extension of Jesus hands and feet.

She lives a lifestyle of priestly prayer, worship, hospitality, faith and victory.

Ann's mystical writings carry the fragrance of the fresh wine of encounter with her Lord.

I recommend you dive into this book and enjoy the feast that it is.

Milly Bennitt-Young

Cabin Academy

INTRODUCTION

To trust in the Ancient of the Ancients, the supreme being that is beyond past, beyond "let there be light", the I AM!.

When the created and the Creator stand as one, this 'one' becomes the tree that is planted by the living waters, extending its roots beyond the cosmos, beyond the seen and unseen, beyond the created to the altar where the Lamb was slain before the creation of the worlds. This is the divine dwelling of sons ~ in Him, for Him and through Him. Yet, just like a tree that has endured many harsh seasons, carrying within the memories that testify to them, so has been the journey of sons.

We awaken in our divine nature in Him. Then the memory of the fall and its consequences start to whisper of their own journeys and unredeemed encounters. We either run away condemned or choose to journey inward - to know us, to Christ in us and awaken that redemption song in the depths of us. We journey inward to trade those ashed memories for beauty, memories that have already been covered in Calvary. We remember that we are only separated from these waters in our present awareness. These are musings of remembering.

ANN WANGARI

JOY

And then I found freedom
in the altar of surrender.
Delight was one of the flames
that consumed the altar
and everything in it.
So I clung to delight and
allowed it to transform
my weakness into
His joyous strength.

JOY

As you follow the Lamb wherever He goes,

    the fear of crucifixion

    scatters in your embrace of the cross.

As you continuously lay down your life

    so that the life of Yeshua

    may be made manifest through you,

He will become the joy you find

    in the midst of any tribulation.

He will be your all in all in every season.

Be present in your current situation and He will meet
you there.

Be real to yourself as you journey.

Where you are now in your spiritual adventure is where He will
meet you if you allow Him.

Not where you will pretend to be or hope to be just because
you want to identify with others who are in a different
step in their journey.

Remember He can not be fooled, so be authentic and give Him
what you presently are.

An honest weak soul, abandoned with complete faith in His
mercy and strength, can achieve more in Him than an
army armed with its own strength.

Endeavor to get lost in His eyes until you are found in
dimensions of His heart, and there you will see all things
as they are in Him.

It is a humbling thing when His presence invades a tent of meeting when we fellowship. However, do not let your thirst to be so shallow that you only skip from one meeting to another so that you only taste of His presence when you miss Him (although there is a place for that when you are new in the faith). He desires more than just a visitation. Go on your knees until your desperation to see His face is awakened.

"Oh the joy of creating a sanctuary

in our hearts for Him to dwell".

When the revelation of

"without His manifested presence every day you have nothing"

is awakened in the depths of your being,

then comes the habitation.

The reality of Christ in you,

manifesting through you and around you,

as you become like the One you behold.

Even in our heights of experiencing the bliss of His joy,

He is still more real than our experience.

There is still more height and depths to go!

His incommunicable nature is more real than

our expressive language.

His very life breathed through your lips is the continuous

inhaling and exhaling of life Himself.

Be In love with Love Himself.

JOY

Darling! Step in the crimson love of His blood and let go. Let go of the right to be right, of your pride, fear of men, the need to please anyone, your culture and doctrines that do not reflect kingdom culture, and anything in you that tries to block His divine light in you. In that altar where the lamb was slain for your redemption, patiently wait for Him there.

YES!

Even though your humanness will be lamenting the loss of all that did not stand in the furnace of His purification, know that He can never be deaf to a broken spirit.

Wait for Him as your Cornerstone.

When He comes, everything that you have traded in the sea of His Blood will be redeemed and transfigured in the light of His glory.

To a love that is awakened every minute is an adventure.

To the sleeping beauty to pursue Him just because of love is

not enough.

Unless she wants something from Him, pursuit is time wasting

in her eyes.

Those who even dare open the door to love and say yes to all

its influence seem a great fool to the sleeping one.

Which dignity are you willing to protect at the cost of your

union with all in all?

Ask Him to make you the most joyous fool and to find delight

in using your foolishness to confound the wise

around you.

JOY

In your pursuit you will find yourself trying to balance busyness and longing to escape and be with Him. There will be seasons where more of you will be demanded than ever and the longing to spend more time in the secret place will become an ache. You really miss Him so much ~ the lover of your soul. Remember that He is not gone, He is there and actually making your busy day joyous with His intoxicating presence. Just surrender trying. There will be times that He will want you to retreat alone with Him. There will be a time in maturing that He will teach you how to be completely blissfully in His rest, no matter how intense life will ever become, and still feel the warmth of the eye that moves to and from the earth seeking. There are sensations of joy, strength and gladdening peace in knowing that even when doing the mundane and hard work you have already been found in Him. His attention is on you and there is grace to be fully blissed as a victim of divine love.

Rise up, O God, and scatter your enemies! (Psalm 68:1). He will indeed arise and scatter them - but remember the real enemy is within and the devil has already been defeated. So what enemies? It is no longer the enemies out there but those habits that drive you further away from Him as your first love. The lukewarmness, the pride, self-pity, unbelief, hate, gossip, judgmental spirit, hypocrisy etc. What does it look like when He scatter these enemies? If He needs to rise up in you then all the wrong foundations will be shaken in the scattering. It is not a time of calmness. When, in His Mercy, He awakens the need and desperation for you to know, really know Him, you start to hate everything that was standing in your way. When you fall from pride, His grace becomes the hands in which you fall. In that place He embarks you on a journey of humility and trust.

Know Love cares this much and longs to be known, embraced and expressed in you. Then you will find joy in telling Him every day to arise in you and scatter His enemies.

Like musical notes on a piece of paper is His healing breath

   on leaves of the Tree of Life.

Oh the joy of transcendent life, ever feeding of that tree and

   ever drinking from a river that has touched the

   throne of God and of the Lamb.

Out of Zion healing comes through those who have

   learned to feast and to inhale the

   healing breath of the true vine.

You will exhale His life wherever you are sent

   and that is the longing of all creation.

The bliss of vulnerability only lingers so sweet if you who have embraced the pace of freedom. To know the joy of laughter, the agony of sorrow, the streams of tears from one who has been broken - only to be kissed back to wholeness by life Himself. To bend so low, like a seed to be crushed until the oil flows, but still have the inner cry for more of Him even if it means more dying. The groaning in longing for eternity within to manifest, the awakened dreams to prosper, to share the hope of glory in you to the hopeless and for Him to become your glory. To cling to His ways even when your ego is screaming. Rest is in knowing the source of streams is in Him and it's in Him that you live, move and have your being. Oh, the joy of knowing His whispers between the storms, the gentle wave that says this light affliction which is but for a moment, works for us a far more exceeding and eternal weight of glory (2 Cor 4:17 KJV). For it is in that moment when you remember that this is a journey and He is the Way. When you have beheld life Himself, fear becomes your past and in every storm you can only sing "it is well..." as you wait for Him to perfect everything that concerns you.

During those moments of weakness,

    when you choose Him over self-pity,

    the lion of your tribe can not help Himself but come

    crashing in through your gates as the King of Glory.

Stand before His face as His breath becomes your roar,

    claiming every territory in you and breaking every

    chain of limitations and fear.

In His boldness you become bold and the endless bliss of His

    wild joy becomes your strength.

His kiss to your weak soul is armor that causes you to arise

    and roar with Him.

So be confident even in your weakness

    when you approach the throne.

PAIN

In the realm of union,
the crown and thorn in
His head become one.
Pain and joy dance
together in the light
of His face

PAIN

Sometimes the new season you are expecting will not knock on your door adorned with pearls and bright lights, singing "here comes your expected post". It will wear a simple servant garment, waiting for you to open the door. It may make itself obscure and hide in the pain and groanings of your expectations. It will look like nothing you expected. Sometimes the situation might turn from bad to worse, just like labor pains. Embrace it through the trust that there is a God who makes everything beautiful in its time. Then the King within you will eventually manifest and with Him is a Kingdom that conquers. You will realise that His intention was not just to deliver you but to teach you how to overcome, rule and reign with Him. It will be worth it.

During your pruning, this fragile dust called flesh will

scream louder in protest.

Still choose to behold Him in your pains, your deep moaning,

as the axe of truth cuts down some of the branches

you have gotten accustomed to.

This might be uncomfortable, but still, choose Him.

Choose that pain that produces immortal fruits over

the weight of the worthless branches.

Love Him as your vinedresser and your fire that purifies.

Broken pieces of your life somehow freeze in a second of

    eternity for the vessel to weep.

The pain of separation from what was and the mocking voices

    of those that can't understand the vessel you

    have become only adds to the pain like poking

    a bleeding wound.

But one that has gone through the process now understands

    that every piece falls into the hand of the master potter.

In silence, like a lamb that is been slain,

    quiet your soul in His will.

When the sword in His hand cuts between the bones and

    marrow, releasing beams of truth and righteousness

    in you, bend before the potter and offer Him worship.

Learn to celebrate in seasons of suffering because we know that when we suffer we develop endurance which shapes our character. When your character is refined, you learn what it means to hope and anticipate God's goodness. Hope will never fail to satisfy your deepest need because the Holy Spirit that was given to you has flooded your heart with God's love (See Romans 5). As you learn to suffer and go through any affliction in union with Him, offering to Him your sufferings and sacrifices and uniting your sufferings with Him, he teaches you how to drink from the rivers of His delight.

In that place everything fades away compared to the reward of having Him as your all in all.

PAIN

You will be afflicted in every way, but be patient. Remember His grace will always be sufficient for you and He will deliver you from them all. In that season remember to not get distracted by other people's journey, nor compare your progress. Instead look inwards to Yeshua who is in you. Fix your gaze in Him even in your darkest moments. When you can not see or feel Him, trust in His love! The love that would hang on the cross for you can be trusted to not leave nor forsake you, even in your most afflicted moments. Do not give up. Choose to endure the pain by desiring Him more than Him taking the affliction away. You will find that your lover, who is also a consuming fire, was kindling the fire in your bones and teaching you to fly. The furnaces of affliction lead to flight!

SURRENDER

Beyond oxygen,
a surrendered breath!
When you choose to inhale
and exhale Him and in Him.
That is immortal.

SURRENDER

"Arise, shine,

for your light has come,

and the glory of the LORD

rises upon you".

(Isaiah 60:1 NIV)

In your surrender to be as He is, and in your journey of many deaths like Paul (1 Corinthians 15:31), you now no longer live but Him. That light in you swallows what is mortal, clothing you with immortality which is Himself. May your longings intensify until you are transfigured into your Heavenly dwelling(s), here on earth as it is in Heaven.

When you approach His throne, linger long enough to learn from the elders who rightfully wear their crowns. They are wise enough to know that, before Him, there is only One who keeps the crown. They joyfully cast their crowns before Him as they fall down in worship and adoration. Receive grace to know that if we approach Him with our hearts wrapped in our given titles or our accomplishments and not as a worshiper, then we choose to keep our crowns on. So cast it all at his feet and join the glorious assembly that is gathered around Him. There you will find your king waiting and rejoicing over your presence. So zealously run to Him with your gaze fixated in His face. Surrender your all without reservation until you become invisible in the glory, with only Him (Christ in you) visibly manifesting in you and through you.

SURRENDER

Desire to understand the ways of silence

and you will find silence whole and complete

in its expression.

It is a frequency higher and more harmonising than

any tongues of men.

If you linger in its contemplative state, you will find

that even a stubborn soul stumbles and falls

in surrender to its charm.

Even a fool is considered wise when silence is present.

So learn to stand in silence before the author of many

languages and behold Him in that light until

the mystery of silence is provoked in you.

Remember that He is all things and mystery is His name.

He may be a man of war who stirs up zeal and triumph

over His enemies but He is also a passionate lover

with un-relentless zeal to pursue you until you

surrender to His love.

Embrace Him as your thirst and also your satisfaction.

Beautiful is a soul that has surrendered to His mysteries

and is sensitive to His touch.

Don't forget to remember that you are deeply loved!

That you are not alone. Look around and see the great Cloud of Witnesses cheering you as you take another step towards the goal. Many are for you. What is against you is irrelevant compared to Yahweh, who is dancing over you as you overcome in Him. So laugh! Laugh, even in the whispers of weakness because in that place you will find Him as your strength. Be that love that you already are in Him to all creation. Roar if you must. Break the chains of captivity. Let His zeal and passions capture you, pursue you until you surrender to the One. The king is captivated by your beauty, so remember to just be, and in the stillness, He will remind you of that song - your song.

Take a walk alone in nature and let it teach you. Look at the undisturbed stillness of a lake. You will see that it is only in undisturbed waters that the reflection of what is above becomes clear. In the union of the Holy Spirit we surrender to His flow. In His current we begin to reflect the very image of Heaven for others to behold Love Himself. We become more aware of the omnipresence of God, attentive to the marvels of nature that surround us and testify to His infinite wisdom.

This is worship.
Let His creation trigger your affection for Him.
Learn to allow the simplicity of life - like a floating leaf on
your path, a smile from a stranger or silence of
a sleeping child - teach you of His meekness.

SURRENDER

Fleeting moments are like capturing seasons in a living lens. Accept the passing of the old by welcoming the new, no matter what that looks like. Be aware that, in order to go from one depth to another, the demand to let go of what He demands of you is non-negotiable. So turn inward to yourself to minister to your soul, to let go and trust in Him, to stop clinging on the residue of familiarity and surrender to the mystery of the unknown path. The flow of the former is too diminutive to reflect what the soul is becoming. We must silence every excuse to remain in the past and take a quantum leap into the unknown. The journey in Him must continue.

There is beauty in tears from a surrendered heart.

Know that you do not have to hide in the cleft of the rock

until "you have it all together".

He is already satisfied in you, even in your mess.

Right then you can collapse in His arms, feel Him closer

than your skin - even without uttering a word

- and allow Him to clothe your weakness with

the beauty of His majestic strength.

SURRENDER

Learn to step in the altar of Abba's heart and surrender.

Lay down who you are, what you have become and what you
will be before Him.

Yield your ways to His ways, the understanding of your heart
to the reality of His heart, to the beat of His heart.

Yield your desires before His desires in order to know
Him fully and to become as He is.

For you no longer live but Christ.

Desire to be the full expression of His nature as
His beloved son..

To surrender to the very nature of the perfect One is to be

in union with light as a transfigured son.

Overcome mortal tendencies of the flesh by ascending as

an immortal pillar of light in His temple.

For on this altar the fire of His love consumes you

and purifies you as the Holy Spirit quickens

your mortal body.

SURRENDER

Child! Give up resisting.

To return to where it all begun sometimes you just need to surrender to the ancient winds and let its force take you home. When you have asked and heard about the ancient path, always remember it is a living pathway. The path is fully aware of your existence, your story and it knows your song. It has been whisperings it to you and waiting for you to come home and just be.

You don't need to understand it, my child,

> *but I promise you that when you yield*

> *to its ways then understanding will come.*

It is not that you don't know, it's just a matter

> *of positioning and then you will remember it all!*

The majestic whisper birthed from the womb of the divine

is ever so soft to the soul.

A whisper so soft to the soul that bends and surrenders

it's own kingdom, to be birthed a new from the

divine womb, but strong enough to melt any mountain

and uproot any force that stands against it.

Stand at the cross road like Jeremiah and wait for

this whisper.

If you do not resist it, you will discover that it holds

the ancient paths that are awaiting you.

STILLNESS

Yeshua, keep on dancing
and singing over my
troubled waters until my
soul is restored to your very
image. May stillness of
the likeness of the Sea
of Glass becomes the very
reflection of my being

STILLNESS

There is a language called silence. When understood, in it lies solitude. Songs are echoed from the heart to His heart, louder than words. In the gathering of silence, souls lose reasons to be heard. It is only then that the clarity of the small voice that has been speaking all along becomes, the only voice to be obeyed, is heard. So when He stands before you, prefer to abandon all you know and choose to rather love Him whom you can't explain.

A holy stillness transcends words.

"Be silent before the presence of the Lord GOD: for the day of the LORD is at hand: for the LORD has prepared a sacrifice, He has bid His guests." Zephaniah 1:7 [Jubilee Bible]

Glued to His eyes and forever fascinated by His beauty!

Look at Him, your majestic king. Where else would you

stand, but before Him as He awakens your morning

with new songs?

No one else can satisfy as He does.

The epitome of romance is He!

Jesus, the glorious king!

Desire Him intensely and in stillness - when heart,

mind and strength bend their knees in unison

before Him and He will come and make His home in you.

In the corridors of time is the waiting room of unanswered prayers. Wait! Be still and remain open before Him. In this propensity, His still small voice will teach you how to wage war and take dominion. In stillness, time will lose its power to mock you.

For you don't wait as one who is lost but as one

who understands that to wait is a journey of

learning, seeking, listening and conversing with

the One who transcends all things.

In your waiting He teaches you how to govern with a transcendent mind, above time and space. Ask Him to renew your strength as you wait.

There is the voice of an extravagant father,

longing to be found.

To go lower is to go higher in this kingdom.

This is a mysterious invitation that He is calling

you to discover.

He shouts in the stillness of heart "be still and know".

To be known by all is the depth of His desire.

The few that master the stillness by answering the call

to fellowship in His depths (Psalms 42:7)

truly minister to His longings and are fully satisfied

in His satisfaction.

In the depths of stillness the conscious transcends

beyond senses and unites with the mind of the One

whose tells it to "be still and know, I AM".

When you gain peace in this transcendental state you

are eternally wealthy.

You will find that, even in stillness, Love is still

reconciling the whole creation to Himself.

BROKENNESS AND OBEDIENCE

"It is not hard to obey when we love the one whom we obey" St.Ignatius of Loyola

BROKENNESS A...

It is the broken heart that sings the healing melody.

It is the broken vessel that realises the sweetest

restoration fragrances.

It is the broken ground that produces the crop.

It is the crushed seed that produces oil.

A heart that has been forgiven much now only breaths

to redeem.

So do not confuse your trials or advances with your identity.

Sonship stands the test of time when established in

His love and cultivated in intimacy.

Remember Psalms 51:17; "It is a broken spirit that He

does not despise"

Like a river in search of the lowest place to bring life, grace also flows in search of the deep places in you, with a sound affirming that lower still is the only way up.

The door to His heart is on the floor of your contrite and broken heart. *To go lower is to go higher. The voice of an extravagant lover who longs to be found whispers. Only a few that master the stillness bend low enough for grace to usher them in the chambers of His heart.*

He desire of us to obey His will. To choose the council of our own soul is to silently say again and again to Him "Depart from me, I do not want to know you". Yet in His mercy and grace, He will go beyond our mess and provide a way of escape and opportunities for us to repent, to desire to know and obey Him.

See that you do not honor Him with your lips
*   and deny Him with your heart.*
Love Him now with all of your soul, mind and strength.

When you find yourself struggling to be honest and simple in asking for help from Him so that you can love Him well, and for those moments that you feel nothing, just remember that as fragile as you are the king of multiverse still choose that weakly dust as a temple for Him to fully dwell in. Let that be enough to make you long for your next breath and the adventurous plan that He has for you.

He breathed!

The ever vibrating voice of the One who spoke,

*   still speaks.*

You are a word sent out as good news to

*   the whole creation.*

Sometimes you will need to speak as an oracle.

Other times your assignment will be the language of

*   intentional silence and loving those He sent you*

*   to with your actions.*

Your very presence is a voice.

The eternity in your heart becomes the vibrating pillars

*   where 'Christ in you' manifests as He pleases in*

*   that situation - just because you have obeyed.*

To do only that which you see the Father do

*   is the satisfaction of sons.*

Be slow to speak.

Sometimes an unexpressed thought is like a hidden treasure.
When words spoken would seem to diminish the
>   *value of unspoken, one can only behold that*
>   *unspoken treasure in secret until you are*
>   *transformed to be like it.*
Then you no longer need words to explain the mystery
>   *because you now become the expression of it*
>   *- the evidence of things not seen.*

When pride is confronted with the truth,

    it still chooses self.

The fall that comes after pride is sometimes

    His grace running after the areas of your heart.

Areas that are so blindly exalted and lifted up to self that in His mercy He has to humble them so low and speak tenderly to them so that He might restore you. Those who taste His kindness in such a state embrace repentance. To accept Him is to allow the humbling, piercing and living sword of truth to find a resting place in your soul and establish a foundation where His tabernacle can rest in you.

UNION DANCE

But there were those who loved to wander in the tracks of the ancient winds. Those who could boldly stand between the living gates and welcome the force of the winds from the four corners. They were trained how to dance, bend and even move faster than the speed of wind by the master of all creation. The bending was their yielding and that was unbreakable.
"Those who know their God shall be strong, and do exploits. Daniel 11:32b".

As you behold Him from the inside and fully abdicate from the throne of your heart so that He can take precedence, The Holy Spirit dance's on the corridors of your body which is now His temple. Then you are invited to join the dance in the purifying coals of fire in Father's heart, as Yeshua stirs the waters inside of you. The eternity pool that gushes from the Lamb, slain before the foundation of the earth, become the healing source of everything it touches. Just like it was at the Pool of Bethesda when Yeshua met a man lying there sick for 38 years and told Him to 'Pick up your mat and walk."(John 5) you too will avail ourselves to those in need of a Healer and allow Him who is ever bubbling inside of you to restore them again. You become this Pool of Bethesda in Him as you go and heal the sick and raise the dead in the name of Yeshua.

Allow your soul to be free to dance to its own tune.

Do not dictate its movement through the limitation

    of your own body.

Love your own chaos, those orphans parts of you that

    are longing to be fathered back to wholeness.

See mystery's ways as secrets that await to be demystified.

Entertain its sound, its ancient groanings and how

    He longs for your freedom to be birthed from within.

Let go of everything that weighs down your movement

    and join the great Cloud in their transcendental move.

To live in the safety net or to be free?

The untamed mind dances at any risky opportunity to go discover beyond ancient boundaries. It believes that the latter glory is greater than the former and that is the wing that it rides on. The untamed mind never desires to be understood by the common mind, for it forever seeks after and in union with the One who proclaims "as the Heavens are higher than the earth, so are my ways higher than your ways and my thoughts higher than your thoughts".

So in the altar of sacrifice, it is ever trading its carnal
thoughts with a mind higher, untamed and immortal.

Desire this!

There are times that His ecstatic love over you will

cause you to dance.

The desire to run in nature, far from public,

and have "undignified" dance worship will

overcome you so many times – so do it!

You will soon realise that to the creation, ecstasy of

being is just a normal day.

Normal because all they know is to be real,

to stay vulnerable in all seasons and to bend

in adoration with no cares about who is present

while they gather strength from their deeply

entwined roots.

Honor this and creation will teach you its ways.

UNION DANCE

The sacredness of the day is to find Him in your mundane

as He transforms the ordinary into extraordinary.

You will find that He has a way of knitting surprises

beneath the living letters of your life,

highlighting a moment with His tangibility

and waiting for you to pause, discover and delight.

Dance to the tune of the presence.

Allow His love to stir up thankfulness and expectation

in you so that you do not become familiar

with His ways and lose the sheer delight of

an expectant heart.

LIGHT

On bended knees, heart longing, I cry out to you. Your face I see. Your eyes gazing right back at mine. I realise you have stoop down, bended down, to lift my gaze. You meet me where I am. Even when seated on the throne, the king still wears a servant robe and lower still is His delight. May your delights consume me until I become them.

Communion should be your everyday delight.

Remember Him in your eating and drinking.

As you approach the table of life,

> *let the desire to be entirely plunged into*
>
> *the infinite of divine love be awakened.*

There you will meet fire, the consuming love lifted

> *up as He offers Himself to you as flames of*
>
> *Himself for you to drink.*

The grace to cease all resistance and abandon self to

> *His will is granted to those who desire nothing*
>
> *else but to be as He is.*

"For my flesh is real food and my blood is real drink"

> *[John 6:54]*

Oh, Darling! Do not go in search of beauty in the far lands. It is your task as a son to make every place beautiful.

So baptise to life the ruined and forsaken cities within you, and then outside of you, with delight. Giving them beauty for ashes, renaming them Beulah ("Married"; Isaiah 62:4).

Go and sink in the ocean of grace and get caught up

in its endlessness.

For love's sake, venture into the deep until

you become its overflow, until your footsteps

become a redemptive sound everywhere you go.

You will find that the realms thirst no more for you

have soaked them with the beauty of the Son.

His bride is highly flammable

    and the flames in her blood can only be sustained

    in His divine fire.

She must abide and she must become

    an ever exploding desire of His love.

For the light set on a hill is a walking atmosphere of fire.

The bride must allow the fire in her bones

    to transform every wound into a wing,

    for that is how she will learn how to fly.

The Eagle in her must be awakened

    in every furnace of affliction

The vibration of your inner being is the longing frequency

    beyond the tongues of men or angels.

The immortal sound of sonship within,

    crying "let me out", longing to be revealed.

When the spirit man takes its place under

    the Government of Yahweh,

    then the light has come

    - the light is arising from within you.

"For indeed we who are in the tabernacle groan,

    being burdened; while yet we do not wish to be

    unclothed, but clothed, that [what is] mortal

    may be swallowed up by life" (2 Corinthians 5:4).

Even in the darkest nights of your soul,

    when night feels long and lonely,

    in that place where everyone else

    has walked away, there you will find Him.

The One who promised to never forsake you will be shining brighter than a million suns. When His love becomes the light that liberates your soul then it is no longer a dark night but a night of union. A night when the soul is desperate enough to say yes to be one with this one man. Even the darkness is not dark to Him. In that place of harmony, the dawn that the heart longs for is no longer necessary. In Him darkness is no longer dark to such soul but a time of deeper union where, in His light, it learns to see light!

Like a mirror we see Him. An ocean of words, the breathed sea in every page, so clear and so living that it mirrors the very reflection of Yahweh. As your eyes soak in every word, the living water drenches you with an ignited revelation. The souls that linger long in the sea of His words learn the sound of His waves and hear the voice beneath the waters, calling them to go deeper and explore hidden treasures.

Grace to not only hear and see the voice but also to 'do' is given to those who value the mirror so much that they do not go away and forget what they look like (James 1:24). Every word is living in Him; the mirror is living, so wait in expectation ready to step in when the word becomes gateways to kingdom dimension.

Wait until what was once mystery

    starts to become your reality;

    the Word will become flesh for you to feed.

BEAUTY

Her soul looked like a glass of living lights with veins rooted in the depths of His heart, waiting for her to exhale her transfiguration breath. Just like wiping a mirror, the dusts of illusion and the fragmented projections of her identity would be wiped away by the waters of an awakened breath. The reflections of the glass now mirrored the depths of her origin which was God, the perfected light.

BEAUTY

You are a unique sound,

> *a definition of beauty itself,*

> *an expression of the very likeness*

> *and image of Yahweh.*

Your maker and your bridegroom is fully captivated

> *and obsessed with your beauty.*

You are loved and you are strong in Him.

The essence of the omnipresence is when the eye that gazes

> *and that which is beheld are one.*

"On that day you will realise that I am in my Father,

> *and you are in me, and I am in you" John 14:20.*

Let the Sun remind you of His beauty!

Go out on a bright summer day and look up

and you will find that your naked eyes

needs time to adjust to its shine.

Now meditate upon the One who shines like a million suns. If you can not endure the brightness of the Sun, which is but a star, what of the splendour of the Son of Righteousness? Yet, in His mercy, the Bright Morning star will hold your head high. He will take you from one glory to another directing your face closer to His magnificent perfection - until you stand before Him, beholding Him fully.

What detriment can be for you by choosing not to value what is anchored in His heart? What is mind but your thoughts of the past experiences that you have imagined and believed to be your truth? What is the reality beyond your mind?

Your identity disappears as you step into the One, "the mind of Christ". In this place, as far as the East is from the West, you forget and forgive all that you thought you were. The memory of "I" no longer exist in this dimension. The perfection that you once sought is now but a shadow of the perfect Christ. The innocence of the Lamb and His righteousness becomes your dwelling place and your new thoughts. Any perspective of separation and hierarchy you once knew is eliminated from your mind. The only reality there is union with omnipresent love.

Child! Look at the Lion.

Watch him closely.

Let him awaken your untamed nature,

> *your fierce beauty and your unbridled strength.*

Rise up and be the courageous one

> *I have called you to be.*

When the old song does not reflect

> *the glorious future you have in Him,*

> *you must become the new sound*

> *and roar your way to your transcendent dominion.*

BEAUTY

In the freshness of each day,

    when a page of your scroll written about you

    and for you to accomplish is read out,

    the whole of creation waits for your manifestation.

May He give you the grace to make accurate choices

    so that you may accomplish the assignment at hand.

To walk the narrow path that is not shifted by seasons

    demands singleness of sight, death to self and

    is embedded in pure pursuit of love Himself.

Walk the narrow path in order to bring Him glory in all things.

Fall in love, into love, with Him again and again.

He is the wineskin. Allow Him to expand in you so that you can know the height, depth and width of His love and become love manifested. Love is tested in those situations that you can logically justify why shouldn't become love to some people or situations. But remember that it is your cry to be like Him and love unconditionally.

Hence why you are presented with an altar to trade
your logic, ego and understanding.
Transcend above situations and arguments
and allow the canopy of love and peace to be sovereign

FREEDOM

For a moment she allowed the cold of the world to freeze her emotions, but there was still a seed of fire buried underneath her soul and her ability to hope in weakness watered it. The next chapter was different.

FREEDOM

Remember your positioning in Yahweh that is above time and space, above principality, power and dominion. Let wisdom teach you. From the womb of the dawn you will receive the dew of your youth and ride on the wings of the Bright Morning Star as His messengers read out your scroll. Receive grace and His mercies that are new every morning to accomplish what was written for you to do before time. Let your voice echo from the depths of His heart as you decree and instruct your day to be as it was before creation.

"Early will I seek you, my Lord!" (Psalms 63:1 KJV)

Dear child!

Why are you still insisting that you only want to

touch the "hem of His garment"

when you can have all of me?

Remember that the zealous vinedresser

is also the Keeper of your Flame.

He is eternally obsessed with your beauty.

So forget the hem and be one with His heart,

where life of all creation flows from.

We bend down close to the water to see our reflection.

Your heart too must bend down even lower

to the heart of the living waters to reflect Him.

This is the unchained melody – when the sound of the

waters below is in perfect harmony with

the waters above!

For that which is above needs to be reflected

below in its fullness.

Let your kingdom come on earth as it is in Heaven.

In your bending towards many depths of His heart, you will face yourself on the way. The mortal dust you have accumulated since Adam has left bumpy marks in your path towards Him. So learn not to avoid the triggers but to acknowledge their existence. Out of great zeal to see the restoration of desolate places within you, seek healing and reconciliation. Move on to the next level until you fully reflect Him with no generational defect. For the cleanser and the consuming fire is one!

I know the world has many definitions of joy

but I ask you to lay down your illusions

at His feet and ask Him to wrap you with His truth.

You will find that real joy is not occasional but a state of being. It is a dimension within God that one needs to engage, to honour, desire and be lost in - no matter what is going on in the realm of time and space. When you meet Holy Spirit as the joy (righteousness, peace and joy IN the holy Ghost) you will give up your ideas of momentary joys that fades like vapour and fully pursue the One who is joy unspeakable.

The voice of many waters will beckon you to come closer. A fool will you be if you respond with your ears only. You must behold the fountain itself! Oh, the joy of the living waters that refreshes your soul. He will be happy if you drink your fill but His desire is for you to plunge yourself inside the fountain. Yes! He desires that you step in His depths until the water covers you. Drinking your fill is not enough for you must satisfy His desire first and allow the fountain to overtake you. "Deep calls to deep in the roar of your waterfalls; all your waves and breakers have swept over me" (Psalms 42:7)

Before you ask,

    the ALL knowing is already there

    supplying and satisfying all your needs

    in the riches of His glory.

If you must ask,

    then ask to enter in the Holy of Holies.

Abide and dwell in the riches of His righteous kingdom.

If you learn to rest at the feet of the One in whom

    there is no deficit then, in your abiding,

    all your needs becomes invalid.

Your first and main intent

    must be to know Him and Him alone.

If you embrace a lifestyle of thankfulness, you will enjoy the overflow of His blessings. This is the outpouring of Himself as "I AM". The tendencies of an orphan at heart make one ungrateful. That which was an overflow of goodness is now perceived as wastage. This will limit or shut down your gates for Him to flow. Mercy and grace will always knock at your doors shouting "open up your gates that the king of glory may come in" until those sleeping parts of you recognise their need for Him and swing the doors wide open! When your gates lift up their heads for Him to come in, the force of His glory will overtake your dwelling like springs of water on a dry land.

Stop and look at the tablets of your heart and you

   will find that each stone, each generation

   within you, testifies of His faithfulness,

   grace, love and kindness.

You will identify with Him as God of your journey

   when you realise that He was at your side even

   in your faintest moments.

Remember that He was, still is and will always be

   your helper and your song of victory!

When you identify with Him as a covenant keeping God,

   then all your fears will fade away and you

   can only bow like Jacob in Bethel,

   worshiping the Lord of your Breakthroughs.

There is an ancient peace engraved in the depths

of your heart that is above any chaos that you

will ever face.

Find it and do not let go until your heart awakens

to its ancient sound.

A sound beyond all that is created.

Allow the breath of the age to come to

become your current intoxication.

"Just then the temple curtain was torn in two" (Matthew 27:51). He is the veil that ripped inviting you into Him - the way, truth and life. His blood is your boldness to approach. His righteousness is your grounding as you stand face to face before Him.

The voice of religion will always distract you from
such a simple devotion by trying to "mend" the
veil in your mind and then making doctrines
of "steps on how to tear the veil".
Ask for grace to embrace the finished work of the
cross and cling to this truth.

God has already raised you up with Christ and seated you with Him in the Heavenly realms in Christ Jesus (Ephesians 2:6) and no doctrine or striving can join you to Him

FREEDOM

When you become complete in Him,

any poverty in your personal identity

becomes swallowed up in the

fullness of His eternal splendour.

The ability to walk into the future to engage the promises written there before they become your present reality is in Him. There is a dimension in the Alpha and Omega that brings eternity into present time. Desire to walk from this place. The tasting of Canaan grapes while still on the other side of the River Jordan brings new boldness and the right frame of reference for every situation before it becomes manifest. This is the privilege and legacy of sons.

All because of love?

The soul that does not know Him and the soul

that is in constant need of grace to love Him

more – He loves it so perfectly.

His thirst for the world is like unquenchable fire.

May His heartbeat become the fire in your heart

that destroys everything that stands in His way

– until the only thing that is left in you is

golden flames.

Allow His fire to turn your very heart into the fire.

To go beyond the fathomable, you will need more

    than the praise or fear of men.

So, awaken your own song

    - the song that He sang to you

    before you were ever formed in your mother's womb.

You will discover that it is a melody so wild that it will shake off every fear and any desire to be anchored in the seen. Let the yearnings from what is beyond the created become the fiery wheels of your ascension. When you know that your cravings can only be satisfied by the very force that created you, you will race through the living narrow gate that is anchored in the mysteries union of the Trinity. The voyage to the endless depths of your heart is the unraveling of this mystery.

"There is nothing new under the sun", said Solomon. So why are you still fixing your eyes and looking for answers in the realm of time and still expecting something new?. To fix your minds on things above and not on earthly things is to trust in the One whose ways are higher than your ways. Let your gaze be on the majesty of the One that even the Heavens of Heavens cannot comprehend. Let Him manifest in you and through you in levels that you haven't seen or heard of before. Set your face above the Sun and be in constant pursuit of the hidden mysteries set before you. You will find that the Son is the mystery, and the race is Him. To know Him and make Him known.

FINAL THOUGHTS

When we say yes to our divine nature, and choose the narrow path of becoming as HE is, we find that Yahweh desires us whole (body, spirit, soul) and free! We find the ruined generation's cities within us, groaning and longing to be found and redeemed. Knowing that Christ is in us, we choose to journey inwards, to know Him. In His light we get to know ourselves and, in knowing, we become that light – the light that awakens a redemption song in the core of who we are. In those moments we learn to trade those ashed memories for His beauty. We trade those lies about God that have been passed down to us with the light of His truth. As we learn to surrender to His depths in all circumstances, we are awakened and remember who we really are.

These are my simple musings of learning, unlearning and remembering as I journey.

ANN WANGARI

ABOUT THE AUTHOR

Born and raised in the beautiful land of Kenya, Ann now lives and works in London. Her passion is to see love and freedom awakened. When she is not writing, she loves to spend her time with family and friends exploring nature, trying new food, having long chats and a good laugh.

Made in the USA
San Bernardino, CA
30 November 2018